Helping Children See Jesus

ISBN: 978-1-64104-020-4

REBELLION
Old Testament Volume 18: Judges

Author: Arlene S. Piepgrass
Illustrator: Vernon Henkel
Computer Grapic Artist: Kristen Hall
Typesetting and Layout: Morgan Melton, Patricia Pope

© 2021 Bible Visuals International
PO Box 153, Akron, PA 17501-0153
Phone: (717) 859-1131
www.biblevisuals.org

All rights reserved. No part of this publication may be reproduced, stored in a retrieval system or transmitted in any form by any means, electronic, mechanical, photocopy, recording or otherwise, without the prior permission of the publisher, except as provided by USA copyright law.

RELATED ITEMS

To access related items (such as activities, memory verse posters and translated texts) please visit our web store at www.biblevisuals.org and enter 2018 at the top right of the web page. You may need to reduce the zoom setting to get the search box.

FREE TEXT DOWNLOAD

To obtain a FREE printable copy of the English teaching text (PDF format) under Product Format, please scroll down and select Extra–PDF Teacher Text Download. Then under Language select English before clicking the ADD TO CART button to place in your shopping cart. Other languages are available at an additional cost from the Language menu. When checking out, use coupon code XTACSV17 at checkout and click on Apply Coupon to receive the discount on the English text.

The Israelites

Sea of Galilee

ISRAELITE CAMP OF BARAK AND JUDGE DEBORAH

MOUNT TABOR

HILL of MOREH

CANAANITE CAMP

Jordan River

VALLEY of JEZREEL

Gideon's 300 victorious over Midianites (scene of night attack)

MOUNT GILBOA

TIRZAH • Test for warriors

There is a way which seemeth right unto a man, but the end thereof are the ways of death.

Proverbs 14:12

Lesson 1
GOD'S PEOPLE REBEL

NOTE TO THE TEACHER

Judges–a sad book in the Bible–records a dark time in the history of the Israelites. "They forsook [turned from] the Lord God of their fathers . . . and served Baal and Ashtaroth" (Judges 2:12-13).

The people of Israel had experienced: (1) God's miraculous deliverance from slavery in Egypt (recorded in Exodus); (2) His guidance and provision in the wilderness (explained in Numbers); and (3) His power in giving them the land He had promised them (told in the book of Joshua).

Before Moses died, God promised to exalt His people *if* they would obey His commandments (Deuteronomy 28:1-14). He also warned them of punishment for disobedience (Deuteronomy 28:15).

Under the leadership of Joshua, the Israelites were victorious over and exalted above the heathen nations in Canaan (Judges 2:7). After Joshua died, the new generation disobeyed the Lord (Judges 2:10-13). They lived as did the wicked people in Canaan, married them, and even worshiped their false gods.

To punish them, God permitted enemy nations to master the people of Israel. When the Israelites were genuinely sorry for their sin, they repented and prayed to the Lord for forgiveness. Then He caused leaders–called "judges"–to rescue them from those who had overpowered them.

This became a cycle which was repeated seven times in some 330 years (Judges 2:11-19; 3:5-11; 3:12-15; 4:1; 6:1; 10:6; 13:1).

THE ISRAELITES

(1) Turned from God (Rebellion), (2) Disciplined by God, (3) Repented–Asking God for Forgiveness, and (4) Pardoned by God and peace from God.

Refer repeatedly to page 19. If possible, print appropriate words at each number.

Twice in the book of Judges we read, "Every man did that which was right in his own eyes" (Judges 17:6; 21:25). In other words, the Israelite people whom God lovingly chose for Himself, rebelled against Him. Because of His fatherly love for them, the Lord had to discipline His children.

The lessons contained in the book of Judges are also for us today. We, too, must choose to obey God if we are to have His blessing. When believers forget the Lord, refuse to obey His Word, and fail to live holy lives, they are guilty of rebelling against Him. For this–and all sin–God the Father disciplines (child-trains) His own (Hebrews 12:5-15).

From the times of the judges we learn also of the longsuffering, love, patience, and grace of God. When we turn from Him, He waits to hear our sincere prayer for forgiveness and to give us a new beginning. (See Psalm 106:44-45; 1 John 1:9.)

Scripture to be studied: Judges 1:1-5:31; Deuteronomy 28:1-68; Psalm 106:34-48; verses cited in lesson.

The *aim* of the lesson: To show that turning away from God causes misery and trouble.

What your students should *know:* The Lord hears and answers those who genuinely repent and return to Him.

What your students should *feel:* A desire to obey God and His Word.

What your students should *do:* Correct habits and attitudes which are contrary to the commands of God.

Lesson outline for the teacher's and students' notebooks:

Introduction (Deuteronomy 7:1-6; 28:1-68; Judges 2:11-13; 3:5-7; Psalm 106:34-48).

1. Discipline for rebellious Israelites (Judges 4:1-2; 5:6-8).
2. The Israelites repent and turn to God (Judges 4:3-5).
3. God pardons the Israelites (Judges 4:6-24; 5:20-22).
4. The Israelites praise God (Judges 5:1-31).

The verse to be memorized:

There is a way which seemeth right unto a man, but the end thereof are the ways of death. (Proverbs 14:12)

THE LESSON
INTRODUCTION
Deuteronomy 7:1-6; 28:1-68; Judges 2:11-13; 3:5-7; Psalm 106:34-48

Show Illustration #1

Before the Israelite people entered Canaan–the land the Lord had promised them–God gave them specific commands through Moses. (Clearly emphasize God's promises and warnings–Deuteronomy 11:26-28; 16:1-30:20. At top of illustration, print important words: *Conquer the Land, Worship God, Destroy Idols.* Make certain your students understand that the Israelites knew God's instructions.)

"Make NO agreements with the wicked people of Canaan!" the Lord commanded. "Get rid of them. **Conquer** all the land. **Worship** only the living God of Heaven. **Destroy** their idols. Do NOT let your sons and daughters marry the Canaanites. If they do, your children will turn away from Me to serve the false gods of Canaan."

The Israelites were the Lord's special people. It was His plan that they should live and reign in the land of Canaan, and be great in the world. He wanted other nations to see the people of Israel as examples of those who worshiped the true and living God.

"If you obey Me," the Lord promised, "I shall cause everything you do to prosper. Your gardens will produce fine crops. Your animals will multiply. You will have many children. Your families will be healthy."

God warned, "If you refuse to obey Me, insects will eat your crops. Dreadful diseases will torment you. Your enemies will defeat you and become your masters."

If you had been an Israelite, what would you have chosen to do? (Encourage student discussion. Ask reasons for their choices. Point out that obeying the Lord meant they had to be different–though no one likes to be different. Ask, "Are you willing to obey God's Word instead of copying those who do not love Him?" Name specific acts of disobedience applicable to your students: stealing, lying, being proud, using drugs, turning to cults, witchcraft, dating unsaved, etc. Help them to understand the choice which the Israelites had to make.)

When the people of Israel first entered Canaan under Joshua's leadership, they obeyed God's commands. The Lord gave them great victories. In time, they possessed much of the land.

But instead of continuing to fight against the Canaanites, God's people became friendly with them–even made agreements with them. The Israelite people said to the Canaanites, "This land is now ours. But you may live here with us if you will work for us!"

What was wrong with this? (*They deliberately disobeyed the Lord. He had commanded them to rid the land of the Canaanites. Deliberate disobedience is rebellion.*) Soon the Israelites permitted their children to marry the people of Canaan. They even worshiped the false gods of the Canaanites– idols of wood and stone!

The Israelites *turned away from God.* They were guilty of rebellion.

1. DISCIPLINE FOR REBELLIOUS ISRAELITES
Judges 4:1-2; 5:6-8

When the people of Israel refused to obey the Lord and rebelliously turned from Him, He caused King Jabin (ruler of the Canaanites) and his general, Sisera, to defeat the Israelites. These men did not believe in the true and living God. They worshiped Baal, their god made by man. (*Teacher:* Remind students of the worthlessness of idols made by the hands of men, Psalm 135:15-18.)

For 20 long years King Jabin, the Canaanite, ruled over the people of Israel. Because he was cruel, their lives were miserable. The Israelites had rebelled against God and were suffering for it.

The people of Israel were afraid. As they talked together quietly in their homes, it must have been something like this . . . Women moaned, "We're afraid to go to the village to get water because the Canaanite soldiers molest us."

Show Illustration #2

Young men said, "It is not safe for us to travel here in Canaan. Robbers are hiding everywhere, waiting to attack us. We are forced to use crooked, hidden paths, and be constantly listening and watching for enemies."

Others complained, "King Jabin demands such heavy taxes that we do not have enough money for our own needs."

Many asked, "Why don't our troops fight against General Sisera and his army and set us free from the Canaanites?"

The soldiers were astonished. "Fight General Sisera!" one exclaimed. "Do you know how strong his army is? He has 300,000 soldiers. [According to Josephus, the historian.] He has 900 chariots of iron! We have none! We fight on foot! We do not have a chance against Sisera. His chariots cut down everyone and everything!"

"What can we do?" the people groaned. "Who can help us?"

2. THE ISRAELITES REPENT AND TURN TO GOD
Judges 4:3-5

Who could help them? (*The true and living God.*) But before God would help them, they had to turn away from worshiping the false gods of the Canaanites and ask the Lord to forgive them (Deuteronomy 4:29-31).

Show Illustration #3

Finally they prayed, "O Lord, we have sinned against You. We have done everything You told us not to do. Please forgive us. Our enemies are strong. We cannot fight them. Please help us!" (See Judges 4:3.)

Do you think God heard and answered such a prayer? Listen to His Word. (Psalm 4:3b; 6:9; 17:6; 18:3; 28:6; 30:1-2; 34:4; 40:17; 50:15; 56:9; 66:18; 106:44; Proverbs 28:13. Choose several of these verses and read them slowly and distinctly. Emphasize that these are also for us.)

3. GOD PARDONS THE ISRAELITES
Judges 4:6-24; 5:20-22

There was a good woman in Israel named Deborah who loved the Lord and obeyed Him. God chose her as *judge* (a leader) for His people. When the Lord heard the people begging His forgiveness, He told Deborah what to do. Immediately she obeyed.

First she called Barak to take charge of the Israelite army. "Choose 10,000 soldiers and march to Mount Tabor to fight the Canaanite troops," she commanded. "The Lord God will lure Sisera, the commander of Jabin's army, his men and chariots, to the Kishon River and give him into your hands."

Barak doubtless thought, *Take 10,000 soldiers only? General Sisera has at least 300,000! He has 900 iron chariots! The Canaanites will destroy us! Deborah must not know what she is saying.*

But Deborah continued, "The Lord God will give you the victory, Barak! Do nor be afraid."

But Barak *was* afraid. He did not trust God as Deborah did. "I will go only if you go with me, Deborah."

"All right. I shall go with you, Barak. But because you do not have faith enough to lead the army yourself, you will not get credit for the victory. The Lord will hand General Sisera over to a woman."

Led by Barak–with Deborah beside him–the Israelite soldiers marched up to Mount Tabor.

General Sisera, learning of their movements, growled, "How dare those Israelites think they can rebel against King Jabin? We'll show those slaves they are no match for us!"

General Sisera ordered his army to prepare for battle. Then he did exactly what God had told Deborah he would do: he led his men and their 900 iron chariots right to the base of Mount Tabor along the Kishon River!

At that moment, Deborah commanded Barak, "Trust God! He is going before you. He will defeat Sisera. Today He will set us free from the Canaanites! Charge!"

Barak charged down the mountain followed by his 10,000 soldiers.

Show Illustration #4

Suddenly lightning flashed. Rain came in torrents, flooding the Kishon River. The Canaanites' horses panicked, threw their riders, and trampled them to death.

Barak and his men chased the Canaanites, killing them with swords. None escaped–except General Sisera. He jumped from his chariot and ran for his life. Barak followed in hot pursuit.

Racing wildly, Sisera saw the tent of Heber and his wife Jael. *Heber is friendly to King Jabin*, Sisera thought. *If I can make it there, I'll be safe!*

What the general did nor know was this: Jael was a friend of the people of Israel!

Jael called, "General Sisera! Come rest in our tent." He gladly accepted her invitation and drank the milk she gave him. Exhausted, he slumped down and fell asleep.

Jael wasted no time. Grabbing a sharp tent peg and hammer, she pounded the peg right through Sisera's head, killing him!

Moments later Barak appeared, searching for General Sisera. Jael called, "Barak! Here's the man you are looking for."

What do you think flashed through Barak's mind as he stared at the dead general nailed to the tent floor? (Read Judges 4:8-9.) Deborah's words had come true!

Who was responsible for Israel's victory that day? Deborah? Barak? Jael? (Let students discuss. Read Judges 4:23–*God, the all-powerful One, was Victor.*)

4. THE ISRAELITES PRAISE GOD
Judges 5:1-31

Show Illustration #5

Deborah and Barak led the Israelites in praising God for His help. They thanked the Lord for sending the storm to defeat their enemy. They praised Him for making Israel's soldiers willing to fight. They thanked Him that their roads were safe again so people could gather in the villages without fear.

(Remind students to praise and thank God when He answers prayer. Psalm 71:8, 14; Hebrews 13:15.)

Deborah and Barak ended their song with this prayer: "O Lord, we pray that all Your enemies will perish. Help those who love You to shine as the sun!"

The people of Israel had sincerely turned to God. They repented of their rebellion against Him. So the Lord did not have to continue disciplining them. And for the next 40 years the Israelites lived peacefully, happily.

Are you a Christian who has rebelled against the Lord by refusing to obey Him? If you are genuinely sorry for this and will truly turn to God in repentance, He will forgive you and fill your life with His peace and joy.

Teacher: Allow time for students to search their hearts and let God show them any habits or attitudes which are contrary to His commands. Urge them to turn to the Lord for forgiveness. Warn them of His discipline if they refuse to forsake their rebellious ways.

Lesson 2
A LEADER FOR THE REBELLIOUS (Part 1)

NOTE TO THE TEACHER

After Deborah and Barak rescued God's people from the Canaanites, the people of Israel lived peacefully for 40 years. Then they "did evil in the sight of the Lord" (Judges 6:1). So the same cycle was repeated:

1. The Israelites rebelled against God.
2. God disciplined them.
3. They prayed for forgiveness.
4. God pardoned them and gave them peace.

This time God's discipline came from those who lived in Midian. He allowed the Midianites to be cruel to His people. When the Israelites turned to Him for forgiveness, He chose Gideon to rescue them.

The Lord often works through those who have weaknesses. Because of this, God–not the worker–receives glory. (See 1 Corinthians 1:26, 31.) "If God be for us, who can be against us?" (Romans 8:31). Gideon became courageous when he was assured that the Lord was with him. Impress upon your students that the promise of Romans 8:31 is for us today. With the confidence that the Lord God will never leave us, never forsake us, we need not fear what others may do to us (Hebrews 13:5-6).

Encourage your students to decide how they can serve the Lord in the coming week. Challenge them to trust God for courage and ability to carry out their decisions.

Scripture to be studied: Judges 6:1-32

The *aim* of the lesson: To accomplish His work God will use even weak people who are yielded to Him.

  What your students should *know*: The Lord has work for those who truly rely on Him.

  What your students should *feel*: A desire to be used of God.

  What your students should *do*: Plan to read the Word of God every day so they will learn how to be used by Him.

  Ask the Lord to help them lead some disobedient, rebellious believer to repent and follow the Lord wholly.

Lesson outline for the teacher's and students' notebooks:
1. The people of Israel are disciplined (Judges 6:1-6).
2. God warns the Israelite people (Judges 6:7-10).
3. God calls Gideon to lead His people (Judges 6:11-24).
4. Gideon leads God's people away from idols (Judges 6:25-32).

The verse to be memorized:

There is a way which seemeth right unto a man, but the end thereof are the ways of death.   (Proverbs 14:12)

THE LESSON

Did you ever say "I can't" when someone asked you to do something? (Allow students to give examples.) Today we are going to hear about the man Gideon who said, "I cannot do it." Gideon was growing up in Israel when Deborah was judge. What do you remember about Deborah? (Encourage student discussion according to Lesson 1.)

After God used Deborah and Barak to defeat the Canaanites, Gideon, his father, and the other Israelites lived peacefully for 40 years. At first they obeyed the Lord because they were thankful for the victory He had given them over their enemies.

Gradually, however, something dangerous happened. Many parents failed to teach their children about the living God of Heaven. (We know that Gideon's father worshiped Baal. See Judges 6:25.) Also, the people of Israel saw their Canaanite neighbors having fun at their festivals and worshiping the false god, Baal. Most Israelites wanted to take part. So they simply joined in the fun and soon *turned away from God*. Like the Canaanites, they began to worship Baal. Gideon's father even built a large altar where his family and the community could offer sacrifices to Baal!

Think how the Lord felt when He saw the wickedness of the Israelites. He loved them dearly–so dearly that He had performed many, many miracles to protect them. But they did not love Him enough to obey Him. Imagine that!

Things *seemed* to be going well for the Israelites. But they had forgotten something. They forgot that the living God requires loyal obedience! (With questions review the commands and warnings of God. See Introduction of Lesson 1.)

1. THE PEOPLE OF ISRAEL ARE DISCIPLINED
Judges 6:1-6

Like a loving Father, the Lord had to "child train" (*discipline*) His rebellious people. This time He chose to discipline them by using the people of Midian–enemies who lived south of Israel.

Cautiously the Midianites watched the Israelites caring for their animals. They saw the Israelite farmers planting their crops.

Show Illustration #6

Then, when the harvest was ready, the Midianites–more than could be counted–mounted their camels and raced up to Israel. There they stripped the fields, burned them, stole the animals, and left nothing for the Israelites.

The people of Israel–watching from hideouts in mountain caves–were terrified. Later, when all seemed safe, they sneaked out and again went to work in their fields.

Gideon sighed, saying to his father, "Why do we bother to plant seeds? When it is time to reap, the Midianites will come steal the grain. So, after all our hard work, we shall not have anything for ourselves."

Maybe it will be different this year," his father said. "Perhaps they will not return. Besides, if we do not plant crops we shall starve to death."

And so they worked hard. But again at harvest time they lost almost everything. Year after year for seven years, the Midianites raided the Israelites' fields and carried away their crops. They were so strong that the men of Israel could not fight against them. What a dreadful way to live! This was entirely different from what the Lord had planned for His people. (See Deuteronomy 8:1.) And all because they insisted on worshiping a god made by the hands of men, instead of worshiping the true and living God of Heaven. How rebellious they were!

2. GOD WARNS THE ISRAELITE PEOPLE
Judges 6:7-10

What advice would you have given to Gideon, his father, and all the other Israelites? (Encourage response. *They should have repented and asked forgiveness of the living God to whom they belonged.* Help students to recall Scripture verses giving assurance that the Lord hears when His people turn to Him. See Lesson 1, point 2.)

God wanted to rescue His people. But first they would have to realize *why* they were having so much trouble. So the Lord sent a prophet (*a preacher*) with a message.

Show Illustration #7

"Listen, you Israelites!" the prophet announced. "I shall tell you why you are poor and hungry. I shall tell you why the Midianites have over-powered you and made your life miserable. You have disobeyed the true and living God! He brought your people our of the land of Egypt where they were slaves. He gave you this land to enjoy. He told you, 'I am the Lord your God; do NOT worship the gods of the wicked people around you.'

"Instead, you have disobeyed Him and turned away from Him. Now you are suffering for your rebellion."

The prophet went up and down the land preaching this message. God's people listened and gave thought to the prophet's words.

Gideon and many others realized that their only hope was to turn back to the Lord.

3. GOD CALLS GIDEON TO LEAD HIS PEOPLE
Judges 6:11-24

One day Gideon was threshing a bit of grain which the Midianites had not grabbed. Afraid to work in the open, he beat the grain in the winepress where no one could see him. (A winepress was a hole in the ground where at grape harvest time juice was pressed from grapes to make wine.)

Show Illustration #8

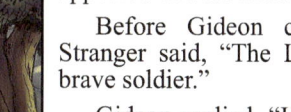

Gideon was thinking about the terrible problems of the people of Israel. Suddenly a Stranger appeared and sat under a tree nearby.

Before Gideon could speak, the Stranger said, "The Lord is with you, brave soldier."

Gideon replied, "If the Lord is with us, why do we have all this trouble? We do not even have enough food to feed our families! Where are all the miracles our grandfathers told us about? God brought our people out of Egypt to this land. Now He has left us. He does not care about us anymore. He has allowed the Midianites to ruin us!"

Then the Stranger announced, "I am sending *you*, Gideon, to rescue Israel from the Midianites. I shall make you strong!"

"Me?" Gideon quaked as he answered. "I cannot rescue Israel. My family is poor and I am the weakest man in my family. I could never rid Israel of the Midianites. No, you must find someone else. I cannot do it!"

"Do not be afraid. I shall be with you. I shall make you strong. I shall help you to destroy all the Midianites."

Gideon wondered: *Can this be the angel of the Lord?*

Turning to the Stranger, Gideon said, "If I have found favor in Your sight, please show me a sign that You are the Lord. Please do not go until I get my offering and lay it before You."

"I shall wait," said the angel.

It took quite a while for Gideon to prepare goat meat, bread, and broth. But the angel waited.

When Gideon returned, the angel of God pointed to a rock saying, "Set the meat and bread on that rock. Pour the broth over it."

Gideon obeyed. Then the angel touched the food with His staff. Immediately fire flamed up from the rock and devoured the meat and bread. At once the angel disappeared.

Gideon was terrified. "Alas, O Lord God!" he exclaimed. "I have seen the angel of the Lord face to face." Gideon was afraid he would die. (See Exodus 33:20.)

The Lord encouraged Gideon, saying, "Do not be afraid. You will not die." (Compare Joshua 5:13-15.)

4. GIDEON LEADS GOD'S PEOPLE AWAY FROM IDOLS
Judges 6:25-32

That same night God commanded, "Gideon, destroy the altar your father built to the idol Baal!"

Gideon thought to himself, *All the people worship Baal at this altar. They will kill me if I destroy it!*

The Lord continued, "After you destroy the altar of Baal, cut down the wooden idols alongside the altar. Then build an altar to Me. Cut up the wooden idols and lay that wood on My altar. Get a full-grown bull from your father's herd and offer it as a sacrifice to Me."

This time Gideon did not say "I can't" to God. He was ready to obey. But he was afraid: afraid of his family; afraid of the men of town.

So that night–rather than in the daytime–Gideon got ten men to help him obey the Lord's commands.

How do you think the Baal-worshipers reacted in the morning when they saw their smashed altar? (Let students give ideas.)

Show Illustration #9

"Who did this?" they shouted angrily.

"Baal will be angry with us. He will punish us!" others screamed.

When they learned that Gideon had destroyed their altar, the mob rushed to his father's house yelling, "We want Gideon! He must die! He tore down our altar and cut down our idols. Bring him out so we can kill him!"

Raising his hands to quiet the mob, Gideon's father demanded, "Listen to me! You do not need to punish Gideon. Let Baal punish him! If Baal is a god, he does not need your help. He can take care of himself and punish the one who smashed his altar! What an insult for you to think Baal needs your help!" (*Teacher:* Emphasize that a god which cannot save itself is not worth worshiping.)

"He is right," the Baal-worshipers agreed. "When the Israelites see what Baal does to Gideon, they will know that Baal is the one to be worshiped."

So they waited and waited. What happened? (*Nothing.*) Why? (*An idol is a worthless nothing. It can never do anything.* See Psalm 135: 15-17.)

Since Baal could not help the people, were they ready to follow Gideon as their leader? We shall learn the answer to this in our next session.

Can we learn for ourselves some lessons from Gideon? (Encourage student response. If possible, write suggestions on chalk board.) For example:

1. For His work, God uses *ordinary*–even weak–people who trust and obey Him. He can use you and me.
2. Gideon relied on God's promise of strength and help. When the Lord asks us to do something for Him, we have the promise of His strength in place of our weakness (2 Corinthians 12:9-10).
3. Even though Gideon was frightened, he obeyed God. (Read Acts 5:29 and Romans 8:31 aloud.)
4. The Lord honored Gideon for the stand he took. (Read God's promise to us in John 12:26.)

I do not know how God wants to use you. I do know He wants each of His children to be ready and willing to serve Him. (See Romans 12:1-2; compare 1 Corinthians 6:19-20.)

For His service, the Lord often chooses ordinary people so HE will receive all the glory for what is done. (See 1 Corinthians 1:26-31.)

Ask God to show you how and where you can serve Him this week. Do you know any Christian believer who is disobeying the Lord? A disobedient, rebellious Christian sooner or later will he disciplined by his heavenly Father. Only when the rebellious one repents and seeks the forgiveness of God, can he know true joy. Maybe the Lord wants you to lead that rebellious person hack to Him. If He has chosen to use you, ask Him for courage to do His work. Are you willing, as Gideon was, to obey the Lord? If so, God will give you strength and ability to do even His most difficult work.

Scripture to be studied: Judges 6:33-8:32

Lesson 3
A LEADER FOR THE REBELLIOUS (Part 2)

The *aim* of the lesson: To show that the power of God can help us in every circumstance of life.

What your students should *know*: God cares for us. He wants us to trust Him and not be afraid.

What your students should *feel*: A confident trust in God.

What your students should *do*: Memorize Psalm 56:3 or this part of Isaiah 12:2: "Behold, God is my salvation; I will trust and not be afraid."

Lesson outline for the teacher's and students' notebooks:

1. Gideon fails to trust God (Judges 6:33-40).
2. God chooses Gideon's army (Judges 7:1-6).
3. God gives faith to Gideon (Judges 7:7-15).
4. God gives victory to Gideon's army (Judges 7:16-25).

The verse to be memorized:

There is a way which seemeth right unto a man, but the end thereof are the ways of death. (Proverbs 14:12)

NOTE TO THE TEACHER

Review the cycle of the experiences of the Israelites.

1. **The Israelites rebelled against God.**
2. **God disciplined them.**
3. **They prayed for forgiveness.**
4. **God pardoned them and gave them peace.**

Point out that God was *again* ready to forgive and restore His people when they truly repented.

For His service, the Lord needs people who are filled with faith–not fear. Satan often causes believers to question whether or not they are in God's will. They are like Gideon who had the same problem: his faith was not constant. Sometimes he was uncertain; at other times he had perfect confidence. We see the Lord's patience in repeatedly giving signs to Gideon to strengthen his faith.

When Gideon finally trusted in the power of God, he saw the Lord perform a great miracle for the Israelites–rescuing them from their enemies, the Midianites.

Lack of faith is the root of fear. (See 1 John 4:18.) Our fears keep us from being useful for God. Psalm 56:3 (or Isaiah 12:2) is the remedy. Ask the Lord to help you trust Him completely in every situation.

THE LESSON

Do you remember the difficult task God gave Gideon? (*Teacher:* Review Lesson 2, part 4. Point out that often the hardest place to serve the Lord is in and around our own home.)

Gideon had the courage to smash the altar of Baal because he believed God had commanded him to do so. And he trusted the Lord for help.

1. GIDEON FAILS TO TRUST GOD
Judges 6:33-40

It was again time to reap in Israel. Every farmer hoped the Midianites would not steal their crops this year.

But there they came! Their army was larger than ever! Certain other enemies of the Israelites had joined the Midianites this time. In all, there were 135,000 soldiers. (See Judges 8:10.)

The Israelites wailed, "We'll lose our harvest again! What can we do? Oh, what *can* we do?"

But what had the Lord told Gideon when he was threshing his grain in the winepress? (Review Lesson 2, part 3. *God promised He would destroy the Midianites.*) Now was the time to act!

Gideon sent messengers to all the Israelite soldiers: "Come join me! We shall fight against our enemies!" All the men of Israel had heard about Gideon. Immediately 32,000 soldiers responded.

Meanwhile, Gideon lost his courage. He thought, *I wish I could be certain that God really wants me to lead the army against our enemies*.

Do you remember what the Lord did at the winepress when He promised that Gideon would defeat the Midianites? (*He sent fire to consume the meat and bread.*)

Now instead of having perfect trust in God, Gideon asked Him for yet another sign. "O God," he prayed, "if You are going to use me to save my people, please prove it to me. I shall put out a fleece (sheep skin) on the ground tonight. In the morning, if the *earth* around it is *dry* and the fleece is *wet*, I shall know for certain that You are going to help me."

(*Teacher:* Explain that fleece is the coat of wool from sheep or other animals. If this would be unclear, use some cloth which will absorb water to illustrate Gideon's test.)

Why did Gideon question the Lord of Heaven and earth?

Show Illustration #10

The next morning Gideon hurried out to see the fleece. What do you think he found? (Let students respond. Read Judges 6:38.) He squeezed the fleece and wrung out a whole bowlful of water.

What should Gideon do now? (Discuss. *Trust God and act.*)

Alas, Gideon still did not trust the Lord. "O God," he prayed, "please do not be angry with me. Give me one more sign. Tonight I shall put out the fleece again. This time, make the earth wet all around, but keep the fleece dry. Then I shall not be afraid to fight that great Midianite army."

What do you think Gideon found the next morning? (Let students respond. Read Judges 6:40.) He found a perfectly dry fleece–surrounded by dew-soaked earth.

How patiently God answered Gideon's prayers! If only–instead of being afraid–Gideon had trusted the Lord perfectly.

2. GOD CHOOSES GIDEON'S ARMY
Judges 7:1-6

Finally, hoping God was with him, Gideon led his army of 32,000 to the hills surrounding the Midianite camp. The Israelite soldiers gazed at their enemy, camped in the valley below. The soldiers thought, *What an army! The Midianites have four times more soldiers than we do–and too many camels to count.* (See Judges 7:12.)

God spoke to Gideon. "Gideon, you have too many men in your army."

Gideon thought, *Too many! Our army is much, much smaller than that of the Midianites!*

God knew what Gideon was thinking. "If you defeat the Midianites with such a big army, your people will think they themselves did it," said God. "After the battle I want them to remember that it was I who gave them the victory."

The Lord explained how Gideon was to make his army smaller. Following God's orders, Gideon said to his men, "If any of you are afraid to fight, leave us now and go home!"

Gideon was terrified as he watched his men leave by hundreds and thousands! It seemed as if his whole army was turning back. Altogether 22,000 went home! Now only 10,000 men remained.

Gideon talked to the Lord about his troops. "You told me to release the frightened soldiers. Now I have only 10,000 men to fight that huge Midianite army in the valley. This is impossible!"

God answered, "There are still too many in your army."

Too many! thought Gideon. *The Midianite army has thousands and thousands more than we do.*

The Lord commanded, "Take your men down to the brook and watch them as they drink water."

Gideon obeyed.

Show Illustration #11

Most of the men put their mouths right down into the water and drank. But 300 soldiers cupped water in their hands. They brought it up to their mouths and–like dogs–lapped it, as they kept watch for an enemy who might appear.

"Gideon, with these 300 men I shall conquer the Midianites," God promised. "Send the others to their tents."

Gideon did not argue. He knew that the Lord–who had patiently given him three signs–would rescue the Israelites from their enemies. (Review the signs: The fire which consumed his food, the two signs with the fleece.) So Gideon finally, fully obeyed God.

3. GOD GIVES FAITH TO GIDEON
Judges 7:7-15

How would you have felt if you'd been in Gideon's place? He had 300 inexperienced men to fight against 135,000 well-trained soldiers. (Encourage discussion. Point out that the unknown often makes us frightened even when we are trusting God.)

Gideon knew the Lord had promised to rescue the Israelites from their enemies. But he did not know *how* He would do it. God knew Gideon was frightened. (*Teacher:* Emphasize the omniscience of God.)

That night the Lord said, "Gideon, since you are scared, take your servant with you and sneak down to the Midianite camp. When you hear what they are saying, you will no longer be afraid. Instead, you will be eager to attack them."

Even though Gideon did not ask for it, God was giving one more sign to this man who could not trust Him perfectly. How lovingly and patiently the Lord strengthened poor, weak Gideon!

Creeping in the darkness, Gideon and his servant edged their way toward the enemy camp. The horde of soldiers covered the whole valley.

Show Illustration #12

Suddenly, Gideon and his man heard someone talking. Breathlessly, they pressed their ears to the tent and listened.

One of the soldiers was saying, "I had the strangest dream. A huge loaf of barley bread came tumbling into our camp. It hit our tent and knocked it flat."

Another soldier explained, "That can mean only one thing. Gideon is bringing some soldiers to fight us. He will win because God is with him!"

How do you think Gideon felt when he heard this? (Discuss. Read Judges 7:15. *Gideon was thankful to the Lord; eager to attack the Midianites; courageous.*)

(*Teacher:* Emphasize the perfect timing of God in this incident. Even in our day He orders circumstances to confirm His leading in our lives.)

4. GOD GIVES VICTORY TO GIDEON'S ARMY
Judges 7:16-25

Hurrying back to his men, Gideon shouted, "Wake up! Tonight the Lord will give us victory over the Midianites!"

The 300 soldiers snapped to attention. Gideon gave to each a trumpet, an empty clay pot, a torch. What strange weapons! But Gideon was following God's commands. And God's ways are higher than our ways. (See Isaiah 55:8-9.)

"Put your torch inside your clay pot," Gideon commanded. "We are going to attack the Midianites while they are sleeping. Be quiet! We do not want anyone to see us or hear us as we approach their camp."

Then Gideon ordered 100 soldiers: "Take your position at one side of the Midianite camp." To another hundred, he commanded: "Move to the other side of the encampment." "Go behind the camp," he told the other 100.

"Follow me and do as I do," Gideon commanded. "When I blow my trumpet, blow yours and instantly smash your clay pots. Then wave your torches and shout, 'The sword of the Lord and of Gideon!'"

Late that night the men of Israel filed noiselessly into position. All was quiet in the Midianite camp. For seven (7) years they had come up to Israel and taken everything they wanted. Now they were ready to do so again. No one in the Midianite army was afraid–no one except the soldier who had the dream and his friend!

Suddenly the Midianite troops were awakened by blasting

trumpets. Then a terrible crash!

Show Illustration #13

The Midianites scrambled from their tents. To their dismay, they were surrounded by torch lights! They heard men shouting, "The sword of the Lord and of Gideon!"

Thinking a huge army was attacking, the Midianite soldiers panicked. Instead of fighting, they ran. There was only one way to go–back toward their own land. In their confusion the Midianite men fought and killed each other. Gideon and his men chased and totally destroyed the Midianite army!

Having won such a tremendous victory, the Israelites wanted to make Gideon their king. But he exclaimed, "No, I shall not rule over you! Neither will my son rule over you. THE LORD GOD WILL RULE OVER YOU! It is He who gave us the victory." Gideon remembered–to his shame–that he had been weak and fearful.

After this battle, Gideon lived 40 years. And the Israelites enjoyed peace–peace with God and peace with others. None of their enemies bothered them.

The Lord knows that certain experiences will make us afraid. That is why He tells us to trust Him instead of being afraid. (Help students to memorize Psalm 56:3 or the first part of Isaiah 12:2.)

The true and living God who helped Gideon is the same One who promises to help us (see Isaiah 41:10, 13) and to be with us (Hebrews 13:5b-6, 8).

Review the cycle of Israel's history during this period. (Show illustration #18.)

1. The Israelites turned away from (rebelled against) God.
2. To discipline the people of Israel, God used their enemies.
3. Israel repented and asked God for His forgiveness.
4. God provided a judge to rescue the Israelites, He pardoned them, and restored peace to the land.

Point out that the Lord does not always accomplish His purposes in the same way. To help Deborah and Barak He sent a storm. He sent confusion to help Gideon.

Today, too, the Lord God works differently with each individual believer to direct and help him.

Lesson 4
SAMSON REBELS

NOTE TO THE TEACHER

After Gideon, the Israelites continued to repeat the cycle of rebellion, discipline, repentance, pardon and peace. (See illustration: Inside back cover.) Forgetting God's forgiveness and His claims upon them, "The children of Israel did evil again in the sight of the Lord" (Judges 13:1). This time God disciplined His people through the Philistines for 40 years.

The Lord purposed to rescue the Israelites through another judge–Samson. To Samson God gave supernatural strength which was ro be used for the Lord. Because of Samson's craving for and yielding to sin, he was delayed in rescuing Israel from the Philistines. Instead of being the leader he was meant to be, he rebelled against the Lord. This led to his ruin.

Emphatically warn your students of the danger of rebelling against God. Even the young should learn the evil of dating and marrying unbelievers. Samson's life is a vivid example of the heartache and misery which results from an unholy union. (See Amos 3:3; 1 Corinthians 7:39; 2 Corinthians 6:14.)

Take a coin to class and purchase something from one of the students. Point out clearly that the purchased item now belongs to you. Because you paid for it, you can use it as you wish.

Then read 1 Corinthians 6:19-20. Emphasize that believers have been bought with the precious blood of the Lord Jesus Christ. Therefore He alone has the right to use His own as He wishes. Pleasing God is not a matter of our choice, but of Christ's *purchased* right. Obedience pleases the Lord (1 Thessalonians 4:1). He must discipline those who rebel against Him. Keep these truths before your students as you teach the sad account of Samson's life.

To review what you have taught about the Israelites in the preceding lessons, choose three students ahead of time to represent Deborah, Barak, and Gideon. Have them tell briefly how God used these three to rescue the Israelites from their enemies. Review the meaning of rebellion *(turning from God)*. Use the illustration (inside back cover) to retrace the cycle of rebellion, discipline, repentance, pardon and peace.

Before class, cover illustration #16b.

Scripture to be studied: Judges 13-16

The *aim* of the lesson: To show that heartache and disaster are the results of rebelling against God.

  What your students should *know*: Rebellion causes sorrow and defeat.

  What your students should *feel*: An earnest desire to please God alone.

  What your students should *do*: Examine their lives and repent of any rebellious attitude.

Lesson outline for the teacher's and students' notebooks:

1. The Philistines, Israel's enemies (Judges 13:1; 1 Samuel 31:9; 2 Samuel 5:21).
2. Samson's godly parents (Judges 13:1-25).
3. Samson's rebellious life (Judges 14:1-16:20).
4. Samson's death (Judges 16:21-31).

The verse to be memorized:

There is a way which seemeth right unto a man, but the end thereof are the ways of death . (Proverbs 14:12)

THE LESSON

1. THE PHILISTINES, ISRAEL'S ENEMIES
Judges 13:1; 1 Samuel 31:9; 2 Samuel 5:21

We might think that after all the Lord God had done to rescue the Israelites, they would be thankful always and obedient ro Him. Instead, they again turned from Him. They rebelled by making agreements with the wicked people around them and worshiping their idols. This time God disciplined the people of Israel by allowing them to be over-powered by the Philistines.

The Philistines were religious, but theirs was a false religion. One of their many gods was named Dagon. This idol had the face and hands of a man, and the tail of a fish.

The Philistine army fought with iron spears and swords. The Israelite soldiers had only wooden weapons. For 40 years the Philistines raided the Israelite villages.

Show Illustration #14

Not only did the Philistines rob the Israelites, they kidnaped their young people and made slaves of them.

Why did God allow this to happen to His people? *(They had turned from God and insisted on having their own way. This is rebellion. And rebellion has a price tag!)*

2. SAMSON'S GODLY PARENTS
Judges 13:1-25

In the little mountain village of Zorah in Israel, Manoah lived with his wife. These two loved God and worshiped Him. It made Manoah and his wife sad to see their people bowing before idols.

They were sorry, too, because they had no children. Nevertheless they trusted the Lord and served Him.

One day an angel appeared to Manoah's wife saying: "You have been wanting a baby for a long time. Now hear this: The Lord is going to give you a son!"

The angel continued, "Train your boy for God. Neither you nor he dare drink anything made from grapes. Never cut his hair. God wants your son to be set apart for Him. The Lord will use him to rescue the Israelite people from the Philistines."

(*Teacher*: Explain that a person thus dedicated to God was called a Nazirite. See Numbers 6.)

Manoah's wife rushed to her husband and shared this wonderful news.

Show Illustration #15

Manoah bowed his head and prayed, "O Lord, please send the messenger again to teach us how to train this son." (*Teacher*: Emphasize the blessing of having parents who ask God for wisdom to rear their children. Urge students to be thankful and obedient to such parents. In this way, they please the Lord.)

God answered Manoah's prayer and sent the angel again to repeat the commands. Then Manoah offered a young goat and grain as a sacrifice to the Lord. As the flame and smoke from the offering rose upward, the angel went up to Heaven in the flame. Manoah and his wife fell face downward to the ground, for they knew that the messenger was the angel of the Lord. These two pleased God by believing His promise. When their baby was born, they named him Samson. They watched him grow and saw that the Lord blessed him.

3. SAMSON'S REBELLIOUS LIFE
Judges 14:1-16:20

The Bible does not tell us anything about Samson's boyhood. But like all children, he would have asked many questions. It must have been something like this in his home.

"Father, why can't I have my hair cut as the other boys do?"

"Samson, before you were born, God told us never to let a razor touch your head. He said He has a special work for you to do. You are going to rescue our people from the wicked Philistines who are cruel to us," his father answered.

"How shall I do that?" asked Samson.

"I do not know, son. God will show you. Right now you must obey Him. Never cut your hair and never drink anything made from grapes."

When Samson was a young man he saw–in the nearby Philistine city of Timnah–a beautiful girl. Returning home, he told his parents, "I have fallen in love with a Philistine girl. I want you to arrange for me to marry her!" (Parents used to arrange marriages in that land in those days.)

"That girl does not believe in our God. She worships idols. Why don't you marry a Jewish girl?" his mother pleaded.

His father reminded him, "The Lord has forbidden our people to marry the pagan people who do not believe in Him (Deuteronomy 7:3).

Besides, the Philistines are our enemies!" Did Samson remember that he had been set apart by God to rescue the Israelites from the Philistines?

Samson refused to listen to his parents. "That girl pleases me and I want her for my wife," he said stubbornly. He knew what the Lord wanted him to be and to do. But he did not care about that. He wanted his own way. And wanting one's own way instead of God's is rebellion.

On the way down to Timnah to make wedding arrangements, Samson was attacked by a roaring lion. That moment the Lord gave Samson mighty strength to kill the lion with his bare hands. He did not tell anyone then about it–not even his parents.

Later, when he went again to Timnah for the wedding, he went to see if the lion was still there. It was and inside its dead body was a swarm of bees and honey. Samson scraped the honey into his hands and hurried on, eating as he went. He shared some with his mother and father. But he did not tell them how he had got it. For a Nazirite was forbidden to touch a dead body.

In Timnah, before the wedding, Samson gave a big party which lasted seven days.

At the beginning of the party, Samson told the 30 men guests, "I have a riddle for you. If you can answer it in seven days, I shall give each of you a set of clothing. If you cannot work out the riddle, you must give me 30 sets of clothes."

"Good! Tell us the riddle," his guests insisted.

"Out of the eater came food; and out of the strong came sweetness." Samson was referring to the lion and honey.

The young men thought and thought. But they could not solve the riddle before the wedding. Angrily they went to Samson's wife saying, "If you do not learn the answer to Samson's riddle, we shall burn down your father's house with you in it!"

Going to Samson, she said, "Why don't you tell me the answer to your riddle?"

"I have not even told my parents. Why should I tell you?" he answered.

"You don't love me! (sniff, sniff)," she pouted. "If you loved me you would tell me the answer."

Day after day she cried, begging him to tell her. Finally–on the seventh day–Samson gave in. What do you think his wife did when she got the answer? (Let students respond. See Judges 14:17.)

She told the 30 Philistine men the meaning of the riddle. They rushed to Samson with the answer. So he owed each of them a set of clothes.

To pay his debt, Samson went to another Philistine city, killed 30 men, and took their clothing to the men in Timnah. He was so angry that he left his wife and went home to live with his parents. (So we see he had made a foolish choice in a wife, against his parents' advice *and* the law of God.)

He should have stayed at home. Instead he later decided to go see his wife. When he arrived in Timnah, he learned she had married someone else. Samson was so furious that he burned the Philistines' fields and killed many of the people. At last he was beginning to do his duty to defeat the enemy, but not for the right reasons.

Now the Philistines had one purpose: to kill Samson. Their army marched up to Israel.

"We want Samson!" they shouted. "Bring him to us or we shall kill all of you!"

Three thousand men of Israel went to Samson. "What are you doing to us?" they demanded. "The Philistines rule over us. We have come up to bind you and hand you over to them. If we do not, they will kill the rest of us."

So Samson allowed his people to fasten him with new ropes and hand him over to his enemies. The Philistine soldiers shouted with glee. Now they could take revenge on this man.

But the Spirit of God came mightily upon Samson, making him strong and powerful. He broke the ropes as if they were bits of thread.

Show Illustration #16A

Finding a donkey's jawbone, Samson grabbed it and used it to kill 1,000 Philistine soldiers. Once again, Samson was accomplishing God's purpose for him–rescuing the Israelites from the Philistines.

When he returned home, his people received him as a hero and made him their judge (*leader*). For the next 20 years, Samson ruled Israel with God's help.

But the Philistines hated him and waited for a chance to capture him.

One night Samson went down to the Philistine city of Gaza. When the leaders of the city saw him, they called out all the police and guards. "Samson is in our city!" they shouted. "Do not let him escape. Surround the city! When it gets light in the morning, kill him!" At midnight Samson got up, grabbed hold of the city gates, bars and all. He put them on his shoulders, and carried them to the top of a hill in Israel–38 miles (63 kilometers) away!

The Philistines were furious. They had not caught Samson and now they had to make new gates for their city!

God had helped him so many times, you would think Samson would always obey the Lord. Instead, he fell in love with a Philistine woman named Delilah. (Review Deuteronomy 7:3. Samson failed to learn from his unhappy experience at Timnah.)

The leaders of the Philistines promised to give Delilah a lot of money if she could learn what made Samson strong. To do this, Delilah pretended to love Samson. Every day she begged him to tell her the secret of his great strength.

One day Samson said, "If you bind me with seven new bow strings, I shall be as weak as anyone else." Was this true? Why was he strong? (Let students respond.)

When Samson was sleeping, Delilah bound him with bow strings. Then she shouted, "Samson, the Philistines are here to get you!"

Samson jumped up and broke the bow strings as if they were cotton thread. Samson had fooled Delilah and the Philistines!

What would you advise Samson to do now? (Discuss. *Return home to Israel. Ask God to forgive him. Please God with his life.*)

Instead, Samson stayed with Delilah. Day after day she pleaded with him. "You do not really love me," she whined. "You just make fun of me!"

Two more times Samson lied to her about the secret of his strength. Then one day he could no longer stand her nagging. "My hair has never been cut, Delilah. I am a Nazirite. Shave off my hair and I shall be as weak as anyone else!"

Foolishly, Samson went to sleep with his head in Delilah's lap. She signaled the Philistines to shave his head. When Samson woke up, he attempted to fight his enemies as before. But he was weaker than a baby! What a shock! He had rebelled against God once too often. Now the Lord was not with him.

Show Illustration #16b

The Philistines blinded Samson by gouging out his eyes. Then they dragged him to their prison in Gaza. There they chained him like an animal and made him grind grain.

4. SAMSON'S DEATH
Judges 16:21-31

As the weeks and months went by, Samson's hair began to grow. He had plenty of time to think while grinding grain. Finally he turned to God and repented of his sinful ways. (Emphasize: It is never too late to repent.)

One day the Philistines were having a big celebration for their idol, Dagon. "Our god Dagon has given Samson into our hands!" they shouted. "Bring Samson out of prison so he can entertain us!"

A boy led Samson from prison into the temple. Samson begged him, "Lead me to the pillars which hold up the building so I can lean against them." There Samson prayed, "O Lord God, please give me strength to get even with the Philistines for the loss of my eyes." God heard his prayer.

Show Illustration #17

Samson pushed against the pillars with all his might. CRASH! The whole temple collapsed and 3,000 Philistines–and Samson–lay dead.

What a sad ending for a man whose birth had been announced by an angel! Why did Samson's life close so pitifully? (Discuss: *He rebelled against God by being selfish, disobedient, wanting his own way, having love affairs with un believers.*)

(*Teacher:* Slowly read to your students Amos 3:3; 1 Corinthians 7:39 and 2 Corinthians 6:14. God commands Christians not to marry unbelievers. Warn your students not to date unsaved because dating leads to marriage. Show that insisting on having one's own way is rebellion. This always leads to heartache and misery. Remind them of the opening object lesson. They are bought by Christ and are no longer their own. Those who date unsaved are NOT pleasing God!)

The story of Samson's life is not a happy one. He belonged to the Lord. Sometimes he accomplished his work against the Philistines. But because he rebelliously chose to please himself, he suffered severely.

Do you belong to God? (Remind students how they can know this.) Are you pleasing the Lord or rebelling against Him?

Show Illustration #18

(*Teacher:* Stress that God always forgave His rebellious people when they *genuinely* repented. Emphasize that it is possible for believers to become so rebellious that God's discipline hardens them. Then, without repentance, they will have a life of sorrow. And, when they stand before the Lord, they will endure the eternal sorrow of having no rewards. See 1 Corinthians 3:10-15; 2 Corinthians 5:10.)

www.ingramcontent.com/pod-product-compliance
Lightning Source LLC
Chambersburg PA
CBHW060800090426
42736CB00002B/104